CARING FOR THE
MENTALLY ILL

CARING FOR THE MENTALLY ILL

PATRICIA GOTTLIEB SHAPIRO

FRANKLIN WATTS

New York ■ London ■ Toronto ■ Sydney ■ 1982

AN IMPACT BOOK

Photographs courtesy of:

Culver Pictures, Inc.: pp. 15, 16, 31
Ken Karp: pp. 23, 36, 75
United Press International, Inc.: p. 48
Fountain House: p. 51
Sybil Shelton from Monkmeyer Press Photo Service: p. 63

Library of Congress Cataloging in Publication Data

Shapiro, Patricia Gottlieb.
Caring for the mentally ill.

(An Impact book)
Bibliography: p.
Includes index.
Summary: Considers the complex issues
involved in caring for and protecting the
rights of the mentally ill, whether in
custodial care institutions, state and
private hospitals, or boarding homes and halfway houses.
1. Mentally ill—Care and treatment—
Juvenile literature.
2. Psychotherapy—Juvenile literature.
3. Psychiatric hospitals—Juvenile literature.
4. Community mental health services—
Juvenile literature.
[1. Mentally ill—Care and treatment.
2. Psychiatric hospital care. 3. Halfway houses]
I. Title.
RC454.S4   362.2   81-22018
ISBN 0-531-04399-1   AACR2

CONTENTS

CHAPTER 1:
THE TROUBLED
MINORITY

1

Ever since people began writing on the walls of their caves, they have revealed their conflicts and fears about individuals whose behavior is different from the rest of society. Through many centuries, people whom we today would consider mentally ill were thought to be possessed by evil spirits or demons. As medicine became more sophisticated, theories about the origin of mental illness progressed too, yet treatment and care for this troubled minority remained controversial. While reformers pushed for more compassionate treatment, other people felt that disturbed individuals were dangerous and should be locked up, away from the rest of society.

Today we have shed some of the myths and stigma surrounding mental illness. We have increased our knowledge and understanding tremendously through research in psychology, psychiatry, and the physical sciences. Yet the controversy over care for these forgotten individuals remains. We are still ambivalent about whether we want those who are mentally ill in our midst or whether they should be kept separate. Most people agree that individuals who are severely disturbed should be treated humanely, but many abuses still go on, even in the 1980s.

There were over 1.7 million Americans considered chronically mentally ill in 1980. These are people who suffer severe and persistent mental or emotional disorders that interfere with their functioning in daily life. They are not able to take care of themselves, to hold jobs, to attend school, or to develop relationships with other people. They often require prolonged or recurrent hospitalization.

Until the 1960s most of these people lived in state mental institutions, but, at that time, several trends converged in a movement called deinstitutionalization. In a short time, thousands of patients from state institutions were discharged into communities across the United States.

■ DEINSTITUTIONALIZATION

Much of the momentum to deinstitutionalize came from the introduction and use of psychotherapeutic drugs in the mid-1950s. Patients who formerly paced hospital corridors, talked to invisible friends, or imagined they had a direct line to God could be calmly managed within the institution while others could be treated with drugs and discharged to live on their own or with their families. Use of these drugs led to a more favorable climate and encouraged the development of other, newer approaches in patient care.

Deinstitutionalization advanced further in 1963 when President John F. Kennedy signed the Community Mental Health Centers Act. This law divided towns and cities into geographic districts called catchment areas, each with its own community mental health center. These centers were to offer a full range of mental health services, including treating and rehabilitating all the mental patients who had formerly been in the protective care of institutions. Throughout the sixties and seventies, the belief that the centers would care for those patients suffering from lifelong bouts with mental illness led to thousands being discharged into communities all over the United States. The number of patients in public mental institutions dropped from around 549,000 in 1957 to 150,000 in 1980.

But the community mental health centers have not developed as planned. There has not been sufficient funding or adequate legislation to support the centers. Thus, the burden of caring for the chronic mental patient has not been transferred from the state mental hospital to the centers, as intended. Deinstitutionalization sounded like a welcome change for the patients themselves, but it has, in fact, been no utopia for either the patients or the communities. Patients have been found in filthy, unlicensed boarding homes where they are often the victims of fire, theft, and medical neglect. There is an unfortunate lack of training programs, good homes, and caring people to help the 800,000 mentally disabled now living in American communities.

■ WHO ARE THE
MENTALLY ILL?
Defining mental illness is almost as difficult as treating it. It is important to understand that mental illness is not at all the same as mental retardation. Both do deal with the mind, but mental retardation signifies a low intelligence. Those suffering from mental illness may have average or above average intelligence, but they have severe emotional problems and abnormal behavior. Mental retardation is a permanent condition for which there is no cure, but an individual with mental illness can improve and change the condition with psychiatric or drug treatment, depending on the severity and length of the illness. Individuals who are retarded can develop emotional problems too, and they have been subjected to some of the same mistreatment as the mentally ill.

In the *Basic Handbook on Mental Illness*, Harry Milt, former director of public information for the National Association for Mental Health, says, "Illness is any condition which causes the body or any part of it to perform in an abnormal way. . . . In mental illness, the abnormality is in the mind and emotions and overall behavior." This abnormality is shown by behavior that is unrealistic, irrational, and inappropriate.

While many professionals agree with Harry Milt's concept of mental illness as similar to physical illness, some would argue that mental illness should not be described as "abnormal" behavior. They would use the term "dysfunctional behavior," which means that a person's ability to act is reduced.

A small but vocal minority take exception to Harry Milt's view altogether. Headed by Dr. Thomas Szasz and supported by some ex-patient groups, they charge that mental illness cannot be diagnosed, treated, and cured like a disease. Calling mental illness "a myth," they prefer to say that people have "problems in living."

To understand mental illness, it helps to know what mental health is. Good mental health involves the way a person thinks, acts, copes, and relates to others. Everyone has worries and concerns that make him or her feel angry, anxious, and fearful; these emotions are normal responses to life's everyday stresses. Healthy people do not frequently become overwhelmed by these feelings and unable to function. They are usually able to cope with life, even though it's filled with struggles, challenges, and changes. For the mentally ill, however, feelings of anger, fear, and anxiety interfere with daily functioning for a prolonged period of time. Their anxiety may be more intense and may last longer than seems appropriate for the reason that caused it.

■ EVERYONE HAS PROBLEMS
It is natural to feel upset and depressed after a loved one dies or when one loses a job or breaks up with a boyfriend or girlfriend. But with time, individuals adjust to these losses. For people who are mentally ill, however, depression goes on and on; they withdraw from friends and lose interest in what goes on around them. In extreme cases, they may not want to continue living.

There is no sharp dividing line between normal and abnormal behavior. Rather, it is helpful to see behavior along a line with normal at the far left and abnormal at the far right. Degrees separate the normal from the abnormal; the same individual may shift to different positions along the range at various periods. We all have emotional difficulties at times, and most people have some neurotic tendencies or habits that can be mildly disabling. A person may fear heights or elevators but may be able to function fine when he or she is not in a situation that causes the fear.

Other people with personality disorders fall along the middle of the range. They have a lifelong pattern of behavior problems: they show emotional immaturity, poor judgment, and unsatisfactory relationships with others. The degree of illness within this center area ranges from people with nervous tics to alcoholics, drug addicts, criminals, and compulsive gamblers.

At the far right of the spectrum are those people with psychoses which are very serious mental disorders. They are out of touch with reality, do not follow the usual patterns of thinking, acting, and feeling, and have severe relationship problems.

■ SCHIZOPHRENIA
One of the most common forms of mental illness is schizophrenia. This disorder, which affected half of all patients in state and county mental institutions in 1975, consists of a group of psychotic reactions that can show themselves in various ways.

Myrtle T. is a 36-year-old, severely disturbed woman with schizophrenia. She had problems eating and developed strange eating habits. She also became unusually suspicious about things at home and felt she was being persecuted, a reaction psychologists describe as having paranoid tendencies. Myrtle was never able to hold a job for more than three months, could not make any lasting friendships, and never married. When she was not in the hospital she lived with her elderly father, who was on disability, and with her mother, a recovered alcoholic.

Recently Myrtle suspected that someone was trying to poison her food. Her fear was so great that she would not eat meals her mother had prepared for the family. She would eat only packaged food that she could open herself.

At this same time, Myrtle began to hear voices telling her that she was evil. The voices were a kind of hallucination, but to Myrtle they were quite real. To help defend herself against the voices she developed a system of beliefs, or delusions. A delusion is a persistent belief with no basis in reality. In Myrtle's delusions, she believed that she was, in fact, put on earth to do good. She was convinced that bullets could not hurt her and that she could converse directly with God.

At home Myrtle was always on guard. She would pull her chair back against the wall so she could see everyone in the room to be sure no one was talking about her. One day she and her mother had a fight about what she would eat for dinner. In an explosive mood, she grabbed a large kitchen knife and threatened to stab her mother who called the police and had Myrtle admitted to the state hospital near her home.

During her hospitalization, her fourth in the last two years, medication will help control Myrtle's hallucinations and delusions and her suspicious thoughts. After several months, she will be sent home.

Up until the 1960s, people like Myrtle spent their entire lives in mental hospitals. Today, with the help of drugs, rehabilitation programs, and the support of social workers, many are able to manage in the community for longer periods of time. Most schizophrenics, however, must still be considered chronic mental patients.

What causes schizophrenia is still something of a mystery. Many professionals believe there are structural or chemical differences in the brains of schizophrenics. Research has not shown a cause and effect relationship between an unhappy childhood and the onset of schizophrenia. But if emotional stress is not responsible for the disorder, it can aggravate the condition. Research is also being done on possible hereditary influences on schizophrenia. There is no easy answer to the cause of this complex disease, but it helps to see it as a disorder of the brain in the same way that diabetes is a disorder of the pancreas.

COMMUNITY REACTIONS

Regardless of the cause of mental illness, people are still reluctant to have those who are mentally disturbed live in their neighborhoods. If men and women have been hospitalized for many years, they may forget to comb their hair for days; sometimes they may wear heavy sweaters in the summer, or coats that are too large for them. They may talk to themselves or gesture to imaginary friends as they walk down the street. Because former patients look and act differently from the rest of the population, they arouse fear in the average person.

In the past, patients were treated almost like prisoners. They were called "inmates," and they were "locked up," and eventually "released." This image led people to think that former mental patients are dangerous when actually they are much more vulnerable and passive than the average person.

Most ex-patients do not act "crazy" or violent, or rave as the public often imagines. However, the few ex-patients who do exhibit this type of behavior—usually reported by the media—influence the way people see all mental patients.

A LOOK AHEAD

In order to comprehend fully the problem of caring for people who are mentally disturbed, it is necessary to look at mental hospitals today, how they have progressed from the past, and how private and state hospitals differ.

We will then look at treatment methods, the influence of Sigmund Freud, how drugs revolutionized the treatment of the mentally ill, and the advantages and disadvantages of methods currently used.

Next we will shift gears to examine deinstitutionalization. Is it working as planned or does the public still fear and resist having individuals who are mentally ill in their midst? In analyzing deinstitutionalization, we will see how community resources such as mental health centers, partial hospitalization programs, boarding homes, and halfway houses are working.

A recurrent theme throughout the discussion will be the legal rights of the mentally ill. By tracing some important legal decisions, we will observe the evolution of the patients' rights movement and the development of ex-patient and advocacy groups.

From the issues and options raised in this book, you will be able to draw your own conclusions about the kind of care that is not only humane for this troubled minority but also fair to society.

CHAPTER 2:
INSIDE THE
CUCKOO'S NEST

2

How to care for individuals suffering from mental illness has been a problem for society since the days of Plato, who lived in the third century B.C. He believed that people who were mentally disturbed were not responsible for their acts and should not be treated like criminals but given humane care in the community.

In the Middle Ages, when the mentally ill were thought to be possessed by the devil, they were kept separate from the rest of society. They were confined in monasteries where priests treated them by hurling insults to hurt the devil's pride. This mild form of treatment disappeared by the end of the fifteenth century when those whose behavior differed from the accepted norm were called heretics and witches. They were tortured and burned at the stake in the village square.

While there have been brief experimental attempts over the years to care for the mentally ill in the community, the trend has been to keep those who are severely disturbed separate from the rest of society.

The first asylums for the insane appeared in Europe in the fifteenth and sixteenth centuries. A typical one was Bethlehem Hospital in London. Its name was often incorrectly pronounced as "Bedlam," a word that came to describe conditions in the asylum. In this way the word "bedlam," meaning a noisy uproar and confusion, was added to the English language.

Although the intent of the founders of Bethlehem Hospital was merciful, the conditions at the hospital were terrible. Patients were beaten and chained or strapped to the walls of their cells like animals in a cage. The harmless were sent into the streets to beg while the violent were exhibited to the public for a penny a look.

■ EARLY AMERICAN HOSPITALS

When the colonists settled in America, all they knew about handling the mentally ill was the harsh treatment they had seen in Europe. In the colonies, too, a stigma was attached to people who were seriously disturbed; the well-to-do, ashamed of their "crazy" relatives, locked them up in cellars and attics. The poor were left to roam the countryside or were locked up in almshouses or jails.

In 1756 Pennsylvania Hospital in Philadelphia became the first hospital in the nation to admit the mentally ill. Seventeen years later, the first hospital devoted exclusively to mental patients opened in Williamsburg, Virginia. In spite of this historic breakthrough, no record of early treatment methods was preserved. Historians believe that this hospital relied on chains and cells for confinement, as was common at that time. Up until 1824 the Williamsburg Institution remained the only separate institution for the insane in America.

At the end of the eighteenth century, Dr. Benjamin Rush (1745-1813), who worked at Philadelphia's Pennsylvania Hospital, advocated kinder treatment for the mentally

The artist William Hogarth depicted
a scene in "Bedlam" in this famous engraving.
The women on the right are visitors who
have come to look at the patients.

ill. Yet he did not abandon the harsh treatment methods of his ancestors. Known as the "father of American psychiatry," Dr. Rush believed the cause of insanity was in the blood vessels of the brain. He believed in treating the body and soul together, something unheard of before his time. Yet he used unusual methods to do this. For example, he would strap a patient to a gyrating chair and shake the chair vigorously to increase the blood supply to the brain. Or, using a device called "the tranquilizer," he would harness an excited or manic patient's legs, arms, and chest to a chair and constrain his head in a viselike structure to force him to rest. Since Dr. Rush wrote the only textbook on psychiatry in America before 1883, he was respected as an authority, yet many people were shocked at his bizarre treatment methods.

■ REFORMING THE HOSPITALS

Attitudes toward the mentally ill were beginning to change around the mid-1800s. Dorothea Dix, America's earliest reformer, devoted her life to crusading for humane care and treatment. She visited hundreds of jails, almshouses, and asylums, working with the press and giving talks to stimulate public sentiment and arouse the state legislatures. Through her efforts, millions of dollars were raised to establish the large state mental hospitals, which, at that time, were considered an advance in treatment facilities. From Massachusetts to Mississippi, Miss Dix founded or enlarged thirty-two mental hospitals and helped transfer the indigent insane to them from jails.

This mass movement from jails to the public institutions caused tremendous overcrowding in the hospitals. In addition, as waves of immigrants arrived on American shores in the late nineteenth century, they dumped their troubled and eccentric friends and relatives in public institutions. With immigrants

Dorothea Dix, the 19th century reformer who worked for humane care for the mentally ill.

speaking so many different languages, many of the earlier advances toward humane care were lost. Behavior became difficult to control because, in many instances, the hospital employees could not speak the same language as the patients.

■ A TWO-CLASS SYSTEM

By the end of the nineteenth century, a two-class mental health system was firmly established in this country. The overcrowded state hospitals offered the poor and immigrant insane custodial care—shelter without any active treatment. Those in the upper and middle classes who were disturbed sought treatment in the private hospitals that were springing up. These hospitals, which limited the number of chronic and charity cases they would accept, were able to achieve order and discipline without using physical restraint because they had far fewer patients than the public institutions.

The unfortunate outcome of this separation, in addition to wide differences in patient care, was that the public lost faith in the possibility of a cure for patients in state hospitals. Patients in public hospitals stayed for years while those in private hospitals returned quickly to the community. For the next fifty years, the overcrowded state hospitals battled to provide merely a sheltered environment for the troubled.

■ PUBLIC INVOLVEMENT

It took World War II to arouse public concern about the inadequate resources for prevention and treatment of mental illness. More than 1.75 million men were rejected for military service because of mental and emotional disturbances. In addition, more men received medical discharges from the armed forces for neuropsychiatric disorders than for any other reason. The publicity of the tremendous toll taken by mental illness during the war years caused the public to examine another aspect of the mental health care system: the deplorable conditions in the mental hospitals.

The federal government became involved in the mental health movement in 1946 with the passage of landmark legislation, the National Mental Health Act. It established the National Institute of Mental Health in 1949 and made federal funds available for research, for treating patients, and for training psychiatrists, psychologists, psychiatric nurses, and social workers. This was the first time the federal government had taken action against mental illness, but soon after this, the introduction of drugs in the treatment of mental illness had an even greater impact on institutions. Beginning in the mid-1950s, hundreds of hospitalized patients, who formerly could not live outside institutions, were able to be discharged into the community. Deinstitutionalization, this mass exodus from the state hospitals, accounted for a 65 percent drop in hospital population between 1955 and 1978.

■ HOSPITAL CARE TODAY

How far has twentieth century hospital care moved from the "bedlam" of the fifteenth century? The *New York Times* reported in March 1979 that the Commission on Quality Care for the Mentally Disabled alleged that an attendant's "dangerous" hold on a 36-year-old male patient broke a bone in his neck at the Manhattan Psychiatric Center. In the same facility, the Commission found that a suicidal patient was "improperly restrained." Confined in a straitjacket for more than ten hours, he was fed big pieces of food while sedated and lying down. A morsel of food which lodged in his lung contributed to his death. These two occurrences are not isolated incidents, but how typical are they of life in a mental hospital in the 1980s?

Thomas W., 25, was recently admitted to the state hospital near his home. The police brought him in from a nearby community mental health center where his uncle had complained that "this nut" had threatened to hit him with an old baseball bat.

Thomas was diagnosed as manic-depressive, a disorder in which a person has severe mood swings: long periods of intense excitement and overactivity followed by other periods marked by deep depression and inactivity. This pattern had persisted in Thomas since he was 15 years old. In his high cycle, he was hyperactive, full of elaborate plans to become a college professor, writing letters to colleges around the country telling of his noteworthy credentials. This period would be followed by a terrible depression, when he would lock himself in his room, refuse to talk to friends or family, and sometimes consider killing himself.

In reality Thomas could not hold a job for more than three months at a time because of his extreme mood swings and his resulting angry behavior. His work history was filled with hirings and firings as a short-order cook, a gas station attendant, and other menial positions. He had tried several outpatient programs but had stopped taking his medication and "forgot" his appointments when his depression lessened. He had been hospitalized before, but he always signed himself out after a couple of months, saying, "There's nothing the matter with me."

When Thomas was admitted to the state hospital, he was wearing an old sweaty T-shirt and a pair of ragged jeans. A short stocky man, he had a wild look in his brown eyes. He was loudly rambling about how angry he was at the world and at his family, who he said were "crazy." Thomas received a large dose of medication to calm him. It was shot through his muscle to enable the medication to start working immediately. He was secluded in a locked room, and when he was calm, about three hours later, he was transferred to the locked ward.

■ LIFE ON THE WARD
On the 25-bed ward, Thomas now shares a room with three other patients. In some state hospitals, there are sixty beds to a unit, with only enough room for a chair between beds; in others, patients share a small room with two to four other patients. Thomas is free to move wherever he wants within the locked unit, but he is not allowed to leave the ward until he has earned the right. This hospital utilizes what is called a "token economy program." Under this system, Thomas receives tokens for taking care of his room, for behaving in an appropriate manner, and for attending planned activities. When he has accumulated enough tokens to be able to func-

tion in the open unit, where patients may come and go freely, he will be transferred there.

Thomas is awakened at 6:00 A.M. and told to get dressed and washed for breakfast, which will be served at 7:00 A.M. in the unit dining room. Unlike a medical hospital where patients stay in bed in their pajamas all day, patients in a mental hospital are expected to be out of their rooms and dressed every day. Their rooms are used basically for sleeping. In a private mental hospital, rooms often resemble a motel room or a college dormitory.

Breakfast is served cafeteria-style. Thomas can sit by himself or at a larger table with other patients from his unit. He decides to sit alone since he doesn't trust anyone yet. Breakfast is over quickly, followed by a community meeting which all patients are required to attend.

Each day the patients discuss each other's behavior on the unit. Gripes are aired; decisions are made. Sarah J. complains that she has not liked the food at dinner for the past two nights. John H. is annoying Harry T. by following him around the unit. Maria S. feels that she is ready to go on a shopping trip. Staff and patients alike discuss these issues and make decisions about what is to be done.

After the meeting, Thomas can go to occupational therapy where he can make a tile ashtray, work in leather or bronze, or make weavings. Occupational therapy has the practical purpose of helping patients learn to enjoy new skills, and they can choose whether or not to attend this activity.

In hospitals that use a token economy system to motivate patients, attendance at activities is high because patients want to get tokens for extra privileges. Not all state hospitals, however, use this system. In those hospitals that do not use token economies, it may take years to motivate patients. Often patients are too depressed to participate in activities, and just the experience of being hospitalized can cause a loss of self-esteem, contributing even more to that depression. Consequently, many patients spend their days sitting listlessly in front of the television set or staring into space. After years in a state hospital, patients take on an "institutional look," a help-less, hopeless look devoid of self-respect and dignity.

Even private psychiatric institutions, some known noto-riously as "country clubs" or "resorts," have problems motivat-ing patients to use their therapeutic facilities. Tennis courts, indoor and outdoor pools, and other luxurious resources go un-used. "To get someone to play tennis when he has just suf-fered a breakdown is a major hurdle," admits an administrator of a private hospital.

After lunch Thomas decides to take a nap. Since he was recently admitted to the hospital, he may see a psychiatrist after his nap or join a group therapy session once he can begin to verbalize his problems.

■ TREATMENT PLANS
In most states, law now requires that each patient in a state hospital have an individualized treatment plan, whether he or she has been there two months or twenty years. To formulate the plan, each patient receives a physical and neurological workup, a family history is taken, and the patient is observed on the unit. All the people involved in caring for the patient pool their information and impressions and they all make a joint decision about what therapeutic approach is best for the patient and who will be responsible for the treatment. This plan is then discussed with the patient, who has the right to agree or disagree with it.

Ideally these plans would be reviewed periodically and new goals established. But in reality these treatment plans often exist more on paper than in action. After an initial ad-mission interview, few patients see a psychiatrist regularly in a state institution. With low pay, poor working conditions, and little room for advancement, it is difficult to get good psychia-trists to work there. Consequently, many foreign doctors who do not speak English fluently are hired to work in state hospi-tals. They may have difficulty communicating with their pa-tients, a fact that seriously hinders effective treatment.

If Thomas were a patient in a private psychiatric hospi-tal, however, he would see his private psychiatrist several times

In a group therapy session, patients discuss their problems with a professional therapist.

a week, as well as a social worker who would help him plan for his discharge. The social worker would also talk with the other people who will be living and working with him after he leaves the hospital. The psychiatrist and social worker are parts of the team that pool their knowledge to understand and help the patient. Also included in the team are the psychiatric nurse, aides, and a psychologist. Professionals often outnumber patients in a private hospital. While some state hospitals also have some of these professionals, they are fewer in number and their case loads are far larger than in private hospitals.

In state hospitals the afternoons are often open for patients to join a music group, play ping pong, or relax. If they have extra privileges, they can go bowling or go on a shopping trip. Although it sounds like patients have freedom to choose their activities within the confines of the hospital, most patients feel a sense of powerlessness come over them when they enter a mental hospital.

William A. Weitz spent twenty-four hours on the psychiatric ward of Walter Reed Army Hospital as part of his graduate training in psychology. In *Blue Jolts: True Stories from the Cuckoo's Nest* compiled by Charles Steir, Weitz writes, ". . . I was not 'playing a patient' but was actually beginning to feel like one. I became bored and restless, and a sense of constraint became increasingly intense . . . . I sensed a loss of personal control over my life. These feelings were very genuine, despite the fact that my time on the ward was only to be a specified 24-hour period . . . I resented being bound by a situation which had taken personal control away from me."

After the evening meal, the recreational therapist may talk with patients about grooming or involve them in an exercise group. Or the therapist may start a ping pong game or try to get a basketball game going. After more medication at 9:00 P.M., Thomas will be in bed by 10:00 P.M.

■ IS HE SUCCESSFULLY TREATED?
This was one day in the state hospital for Thomas W. He spent two weeks in the locked ward and then was transferred to the open unit. After two months in this unit, his depression

had lessened, and he was not so angry. His behavior had calmed down. Insisting that "There's nothing the matter with me now," Thomas signed himself out.

Can Thomas be considered successfully treated? Mental health professionals find it difficult to put a percentage tag on their success rate. For Mary T., success is her ability to stay out of the hospital for more than three months at a time. For Edwin S., success is knowing what makes him ill and admitting himself to the hospital voluntarily. For Sydney G., success is taking his medication every day so that he can live in his one-room apartment in his own neighborhood. Success varies from individual to individual.

CHAPTER 3:
FROM FREUD
TO ELECTROSHOCK

3

The roots of today's treatment methods go back, strangely enough, to the practice of hypnosis in the late 1800s. Dr. Josef Breuer utilized a "talking cure" for people's emotional problems. Anna O., the first patient in the history of psychoanalysis, was a 20-year-old woman with a large number of imaginary physical symptoms, a condition that is known as hysteria. Using hypnosis to recapture her early childhood memories, Breuer found that her complaints seemingly vanished.

Sigmund Freud, an Austrian neurologist, learned of hypnosis through Dr. Breuer. He tried Breuer's "talking cure," which became known as "the cathartic method," a technique in which emotional tension was released by talking about thoughts and feelings that had formerly been locked in the unconscious mind. Freud began by using hypnosis to help patients reconstruct their childhood memories, but he soon became dissatisfied with his dependency on this technique. Preferring straightforward conscious contact with his patients, he hit upon "free association." This method, which is used in all talking therapies today, allows patients to talk freely about whatever comes into their conscious minds.

Freud continued to develop and use this procedure, which became known as psychoanalysis. He believed that by analyzing and interpreting what patients said and did, he could help them understand the origin of their problems and become better adjusted to their life situations. With the patient lying on the couch, Freud, the analyst, let the person pour out his or her innermost thoughts, emotions, and desires. Using free association, dream analysis, and such "accidents" as slips of the tongue as his tools of interpretation, Freud would analyze what the patient said.

For centuries, people had suspected that there might be large areas of functioning outside of our everyday awareness. Freud developed this idea of the unconscious mind and brought it to the public's awareness. He believed that many unconscious thoughts were sexual in nature. According to Freud, children go through sexual stages in their early years and can develop conflicting emotions and feelings during this period. If these conflicts are unresolved at the time, they can become trapped in the unconscious mind and interfere with functioning as an adult.

In addition to unlocking the unconscious mind, Freud developed the theory and technique of psychoanalysis and laid the foundation for all other methods of psychotherapy. However, Freud was not without his critics—in his own time as well as today. He shocked people, especially in the late 1800s, with his talk of childhood sexuality, sexual developmental stages, and unconscious desires. While Freud had many followers who embraced his idea of a doctor/patient therapeutic relationship to work out internal emotional conflicts, other psychiatrists criticized and rejected some of his unorthodox ideas and replaced them with their own theories.

Sigmund Freud developed
the technique of psychoanalysis
and laid a foundation
for many types of
modern psychotherapy.

■ NEWER THERAPIES

Today there are more than fifty recognized forms of psychotherapy being used in the United States, yet all types of verbal or insight therapy grew out of Freud's original psychoanalysis. This type of therapy always involves a verbal and emotional relationship between the patient and the therapist who attempts to bring about changes in the patient's feelings, thoughts, and actions, and a lessening of the mental and physical symptoms. However, the specifics of the individual therapies range from the traditional psychoanalysis with the patient free associating on the couch to the innovative est in which individuals try to reach self-realization in a group of 250 people.

According to William Schofield, author of *Psychotherapy: The Purchase of Friendship* (Prentice-Hall, 1960), the ideal patient for psychotherapy has "the YAVIS syndrome": he or she is young, attractive, verbal, intelligent, and successful. Since many chronic mental patients do not fit that description, it is questioned whether therapy alone can help the severely disturbed person. It has not been proven that psychotherapy will reverse or lessen schizophrenic symptoms. Patients treated with psychotherapy and drugs do not appear to do any better than those receiving drugs alone. Once a drug regimen has begun, however, psychotherapy can help improve the quality of the patient's life.

■ BEHAVIOR MODIFICATION

A form of therapy which is more suited for the average person is behavior modification. While insight therapy works from the inside out, behavior modification works from the outside in. This method is based on the work of the Russian physiologist Pavlov. He showed that animals could learn new and unusual behavior by conditioning, a process in which their good behavior is rewarded or reinforced. Behavior therapists believe that neuroses and psychoses are bad habits that have somehow been reinforced. They attempt to change these habits and behaviors first, believing that shifts in feelings and attitudes will follow.

Psychotherapists charge that behavior modification is too superficial and merely puts on bandages while ignoring the underlying problems which, they feel, will produce other symptoms later on. On the other hand, proponents of behavior therapy point out that it works well on those patients that verbal therapies cannot reach: chronic mental patients, alcoholics, and people with unrealistic fears.

Behavior modification has worked successfully in state hospitals with programs in which desired behaviors are rewarded with tokens that can be exchanged for things the patient wants. Even the most apathetic patient wants something: a snack, a personal chair, or a locked cabinet for personal possessions. Patients who are poorly groomed get tokens for showering, shaving, and dressing; people who sit and rock all day receive tokens for going to recreational or occupational therapy. Behavior modification programs show results, but opponents say it is pure manipulation or even a form of mind control.

Opponents of behavior modification take their argument one step further and raise a moral issue: they say behavior modification contains a grave potential for evil. In the wrong hands, how far would some people go to shape and control others' behavior? For example, could we mold a nation of car thieves or child murderers?

■ ORIGIN OF DRUGS

Most people associate drugs with twentieth century scientific research laboratories, but remedies to calm excited, overly active people and to enliven the depressed are as old as civilization itself. The oldest antidote for mental ills, used as far back as 6400 B.C. in Mesopotamia, is alcohol. Six thousand years later in Greece, Hippocrates prescribed wine laced with the juice of the mandrake root to treat the tense and nervous, as well as the depressed.

In more recent times, in nineteenth-century America, women who were nervous used potions such as Lydia Pinkham's Vegetable Compound, a mixture of herbs and alcohol, to calm themselves. Up until forty years ago, the only drugs available to psychiatrists were the sedatives: opium, morphine, and the barbiturates. These worked in making patients drowsy or putting them to sleep, but they did nothing to help their nervous condition while they were awake. In addition, the potential for harm was greater than the benefit. Patients often poisoned themselves with overdoses or became drug addicts.

Elsewhere in the world, however, other remedies had been in use for centuries. Natives of Africa and India had used the snakeroot plant for everything from snakebite to fever and hysteria. This practice went unnoticed by Western scientists until 1952, when three scientists in Switzerland were making a routine survey of exotic plants with reputed therapeutic properties. They were interested in the snakeroot plant for its value in treating high blood pressure. From the plant they extracted reserpine, which became marketed under the trade name of *Serpasil*. Originally used in America for treating high blood pressure, *Serpasil* was found to have a tranquilizing effect on certain patients. It was soon used throughout the Western hemisphere to calm excited patients.

■ MODERN DRUGS

Following the discovery of *Serpasil*, two major types of drugs were found that worked miraculously on people who were mentally ill. One category of drug includes tranquilizers, which reduce anxiety, agitation, uncontrollable physical activity, and destructiveness. People who are neurotic can take a mild form of tranquilizer to relieve some of their worries and concerns or to help them cope with crises when they arise. Psychotic individuals can take more powerful forms of tranquilizers, known as antipsychotic drugs, which also control their hallucinations and delusions.

A second group of drugs are antidepressants. As their name suggests, these drugs arouse those who are withdrawn, depressed, and uncommunicative. They are not like "pep pills" or stimulants, which give a quick charge. They slowly raise a depressed mood to a normal one, often taking several weeks for a change to be noticeable.

Finally, a third drug, in a category by itself, is the simple chemical compound, lithium carbonate. This drug is extremely effective in smoothing out the highs and lows in manic-depression, the illness from which the patient Thomas W. suffered in the previous chapter.

Scientists have been studying these drugs for almost thirty years now, yet no one is quite sure how they work and why they affect psychoses as they do. Research has shown that the brain is a complex of hard-working chemicals, called neurotransmitters. Some of these chemicals occur in specific parts of the brain. Others help carry nerve impulses from cell to cell.

Abnormal amounts of these chemicals may be at work in the brains of psychotic individuals. Malfunctions of certain brain areas might be related to underactivity or overactivity of particular systems of neurotransmitters. If this is, in fact, the case, antidepressant or antipsychotic drugs, which can raise or lower the amounts of the neurotransmitters, might then cause marked psychological changes.

■ IMPACT OF DRUGS

Since their introduction in the 1950s, drugs have had a profound impact on care of the mentally ill. They are the closest thing yet to a cure for mental illness. In 1956, for the first time in over a hundred years, more patients were discharged from mental hospitals than admitted. These discharges were possible because drugs kept hallucinations and delusions under control; patients were calmer and more manageable.

With these dramatic changes in patients' behavior, the structure and administration of the mental hospital itself could also be changed. More hospitals became "open hospitals" in which doors did not always have to be locked. Fewer patients needed seclusion and physical restraints. "Therapeutic communities" on hospital floors brought together patients and staff on a weekly or daily basis to discuss issues and problems of living on a hospital unit. Many patients themselves feel better when they are on drugs. They are calmer, feel more in control of themselves, and become more sociable.

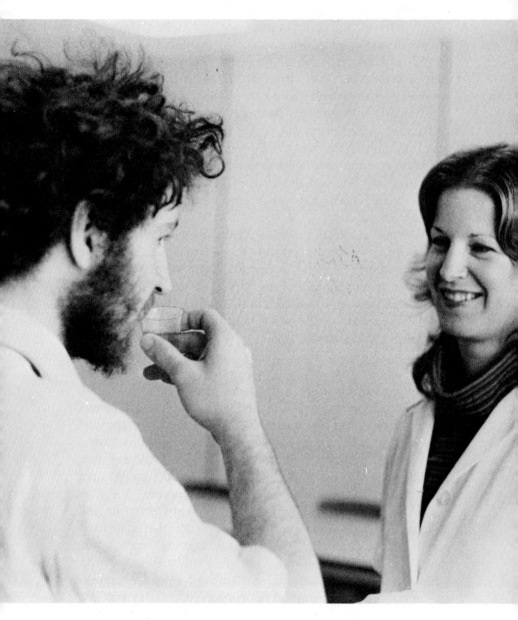

*A patient is given a prescribed drug
under the close supervision
of a hospital staff member.*

■ DISCHARGE INTO THE COMMUNITY

Many chronic patients who improved on medication within the hospital were able to be discharged into their own communities. They were not cured, but as long as they took their medication, they were able to manage in an environment less restrictive than that of the hospital. Administering drugs on an outpatient basis, however, is not without its problems. Patients who have been spoon-fed medication in a state hospital must remember to take it themselves. In the hospital, though, they have not been used to watching a clock or being responsible for taking their own medicine, and in the community they often forget when to take it.

Getting manic-depressives to take lithium is a problem of a different kind. Many people suffering from this illness don't want to give up the euphoria of the high in the manic phase. Eventually they recognize that if they want to lead normal lives they must take lithium continuously to level their severe mood swings.

Another difficulty in administering drugs to patients living in the community is dealing with their reactions to the drugs. Some people experience side effects that went unnoticed in the hospital but become annoying and embarrassing to them in the community. They may decide to stop the medication themselves without consulting a doctor. Then their behavior deteriorates, their psychotic symptoms recur, and they find themselves back in the hospital.

Statistics support this circular process, known as "the revolving door syndrome." A study presented to the 1979 annual meeting of the American Orthopsychiatry Association showed that 50 percent of all discharged mental patients stop taking their medication. Ex-patients' failure to take their medication is part of the reason that 68.7 percent of all admissions to state and county mental hospitals were readmissions, as of 1975.

■ OPPONENTS OF DRUGS

In spite of the benefits of drugs, this treatment has its critics. These people say that drugs are more for the convenience of the hospital staff than for the patients' benefit and that they are used solely to sedate and control the patients. The most vocal opponents of drugs are ex-patients who feel they have been victimized and harmed by the indiscriminate use of drugs. A former patient, Francine Schwartz, writes in *Body Count*:

> *I was given two chubby orange tabs of straight Thorazine, which brought me to a state resembling vegetation within twenty minutes. At the time I was perspiring so profusely and continuously that I began to think that I'd just go on sweating till I died. My mouth got so dry that nothing would quench its thirst. Eventually my tongue cracked wide open in a vicious painful way. My hands trembled incessantly, with a palsy closely resembling Parkinsons' disease. My skin turned a dead yellow-gray color, my eyes became supersensitive to light, and so did all the skin all over my body. I moved in a slow motion, in a heavy fog . . .*

No one can predict how a patient will respond to a particular drug, how strong a dosage is needed, or what the side effects will be. Most doctors try to prescribe drugs that are appropriate, but it is not always known at the outset whether a patient needs 100 mg. or 2,000 mg. of a drug to feel its effectiveness. And individual patients can respond differently to the same drug. In fact, drugs do not work at all on 20 percent of mental patients.

■ SIDE EFFECTS
Side effects are probably the biggest disadvantage to using drugs. When Louise J., a paranoid schizophrenic, started taking antipsychotic medication, she felt restless all the time. She couldn't sit still for more than a few minutes. When she did rest, her leg would not stop jiggling. At other times, she noticed a rigidity in her muscles; her face felt tight; her expressions, tense. Both of these conditions disappeared when she

began taking other drugs in addition to the tranquilizer to counteract these symptoms.

When Louise had been on high doses of tranquilizers for many years she, like 15 percent of all hospitalized mental patients, developed a condition called "tardive dyskinesia," which is a *permanent* side effect. It causes damage to that part of the brain that is used to control and coordinate muscle movement. Her arms and legs twitched involuntarily; her lips, tongue, and jaw were in constant motion so that she had trouble eating and talking coherently. Unfortunately, in Louise's case, when the antipsychotic medication was stopped, the tardive dyskinesia worsened. In other cases, discontinuing the medication may have no effect, or the condition may improve.

The side effects of the antidepressants may not show up for weeks, and they vary from patient to patient and from drug to drug. Common complaints are dry mouth, blurred vision, constipation, dizziness, and insomnia.

Lithium, on the other hand, has only minimal side effects and these are temporary. Yet it also has one disadvantage to the patient. The amount of lithium needed to produce the desired effect is so close to an overdose that people taking it must constantly have blood tests to measure the amount in their bodies.

With all drugs, there are some side effects. One must make the difficult decision of choosing between these side effects and the agony of the disease itself.

■ ELECTROSHOCK THERAPY

If drugs are a debatable method of treatment, electroshock therapy (ECT) is even more controversial. The word alone conjures up frightening visions from stories of the 1930s and 1940s: patients being strapped down against their wills; convulsions breaking their bones; sadistic doctors shocking patients at random.

More than 100,000 Americans a year receive electroshock therapy for severe depression. Senator Thomas Eagleton brought ECT to the public light in 1972 when, as Democratic vice-presidential nominee, he announced that he had received shock treatment for nervous exhaustion and depression. He was forced to step down as a candidate because of the public's negative attitude to both his illness and its treatment. At that time, the American Psychiatric Association issued a statement that ECT has been a highly effective treatment for moderate and severe depression since it was introduced in 1938. Part of the statement read, "In carefully selected cases for an episode of depression, electroshock treatment has proven 90 percent effective."

Today patients receive an anesthetic and a muscle relaxant prior to getting a treatment, so broken bones are a thing of the past. Then electrodes are applied to the temples on each side of the head. A current passes through the brain for a few seconds during which time the patient loses consciousness. He or she has no awareness of what has happened and experiences no pain. The patient wakens after half an hour, feeling confused and groggy. Many things are forgotten, especially recent events. Past memories usually come back after a few weeks, but some patients never remember the treatment or the time surrounding it. Most patients receive six to twenty treatments.

The controversy over ECT centers around what it does to the brain. Opponents feel that patients who receive it sustain structural brain changes and learning difficulties. They also feel that patients can receive permanent, disabling memory loss. In his book, *Shock Treatment is Not Good for Your Brain*, neurologist John Friedburg, M.D., quotes a 32-year-old woman who received twenty-one electroshock treatments five years ago.

> One of the results of the whole thing is that I have no memory of what happened in the year to year and a half prior to my shock treatments. The doctor assured me that it was going to come back and it never has. I don't remember a bloody thing. I couldn't even find my way around the town I lived in for three years. If I walked into a building I didn't even know where I was. I could barely find my way around my

own house. I could sew and knit before, but afterward,
I could no more comprehend a pattern to sew than
the man in the moon.

Like this woman, patients are more likely to distrust and object to ECT and the physicians who administer it than any other treatment method. On the other hand, there are patients who swear by ECT. These people prefer not to look at their problems or confront themselves. They like the idea that their "treatments" will make them feel better and the fact that they don't have to work at it. Likewise, their families are pleased to go along with it. It clearly labels the patient as "sick," and relieves family members of their feelings of responsibility for contributing to the patient's illness.

In cases of severe depression, especially among the elderly who cannot tolerate the side effects of drugs, ECT is considered the fastest, most effective, and most reliable treatment. In an emergency it works quicker than anything else.

Because ECT is so quick and easy to administer, however, some doctors abuse it. In his book *The Making of a Psychiatrist*, David Viscott, M.D., writes of another psychiatrist's practice. "Finding that the patient has insurance seemed like the most common indicator for giving shock; the second is depression."

Obviously, there is no perfect method of treatment. Nor is there a way that is right for everyone. Each method has advantages and disadvantages which must be evaluated by the patient and his or her physician. Then, an appropriate choice of treatment method can be made.

CHAPTER 4:
RESOURCES WITHIN
THE COMMUNITY

4

Once drugs had revolutionized the treatment of mental illness, it was not long before the idealistic vision of humane care for the mentally ill in their own communities took root. This idea of deinstitutionalization was supported by research showing that lengthy hospitalization created dependency on the institution and perpetrated disturbed behavior. Community services for the chronic mental patient would not only cost less than care in a hospital, but also help the patient learn to function more independently. Influenced as well by the patients' rights movement, state mental hospitals all over the country began emptying their wards.

Up until the 1960s, most patients who left state mental hospitals went home to their families. Even with the first wave of deinstitutionalization, only those patients who could go home to a willing family were discharged. Today, however, for more than 50 percent of all patients, going home to their families is an impossibility. Many families are resistant to caring for relatives who are mentally ill, and many are overburdened with problems themselves. In some cases, families simply would not be able to help patients make a healthy adjustment to the community. If fewer and fewer former mental patients can return to their family settings, where do they live?

Decent and safe residential care for those who are not completely ready for independent living has proven to be the most important component in community services for the mentally ill. There is, however, a real shortage of good residential care facilities in communities all over the United States. This crisis, which has been called "a national scandal," is more severe than the shortage of psychiatric, vocational, or counseling services for the ex-patient.

■ BOARDING HOMES

In July 1980 twenty-four people died in a fire in a Bradley Beach, New Jersey, boarding home. The residents, like those of most boarding homes, were elderly, mentally retarded, or former mental patients. They lived on the top two floors of a four-story frame building that had a single fire escape in the rear which they could not reach in the fire. The residents were trapped when the flames spread up the front stairwell, their only other means of escape. This fire is not an isolated incident. Nor are incidents of robbery, medical neglect, and exploitation uncommon for the two million vulnerable people who live in the nation's 300,000 boarding homes.

A boarding home is any type of residential facility that provides adults with food and shelter for a fee. In almost every state with a policy of deinstitutionalization, boarding homes are the most common residences for former patients. Because of the demand for boarding homes, nearly every building used for these facilities was originally designed for another purpose. The buildings range from a high rise in New York City to a converted chicken coop in New Mexico and a mobile home in the midwest.

Called "psychiatric ghettos" by federal and state investigators, boarding homes are not federally regulated and are seldom inspected. Some states, like New York and California, do have progressive laws, but they are not consistently enforced. Many boarding homes are run by warm, caring people, who look after their residents like they would their own children. But for many other people who have no other way to make a living, running a boarding home is a business. They are out to make a profit, often at the former patient's expense.

■ HALFWAY HOUSES

Another type of residential facility is the halfway house. As the name suggests, this is a temporary residence in which the former patients can make the transition from hospital to community living. Although ex-patients do not receive any medical care here, the residence provides round-the-clock supervision.

It is impossible to make any generalizations about halfway houses. Like boarding homes, they vary widely. Some offer nothing but a roof over the patient's head; others are more comprehensive, offering therapy, training for jobs in the community, or groups in which they learn how to socialize and get along with others. Halfway houses also differ in whom they will accept as residents. Since many are privately run, they can be more selective in choosing their patients. They can choose to take only the "better" patients and to reject those with a history of violence or sexual deviation, or people with a history of alcoholism or drug addiction.

Once former patients have mastered some of the basic skills of living and begin to feel more comfortable away from the security of the hospital, they will be able to move out and take their own apartments. Sometimes this takes several months; sometimes former patients need a year of transitional living before they are ready to move out on their own.

Halfway houses, like other types of residences for former patients, are in great demand. Many more patients could benefit from this type of transitional living if more halfway houses were available.

■ OTHER RESIDENCES

Because of the shortage of residences for former mental patients, thousands are forced to live in places that do not have even the minimal supervision a boarding home offers. In New York City alone, 16,000 former patients live without the su-

pervised housing they need. These men and women may live in old, rundown hotels, cooking their meals on hot plates in their single rooms. Some rent rooms in dilapidated rooming houses. Or like the "bag ladies" who carry all their possessions in a shopping bag, they may wander from park bench to train station, trying to find a warm spot to spend the night.

■ FOUNTAIN HOUSE

The first, and still one of the most successful, programs for patients who have been discharged from mental hospitals is Fountain House in New York City. It originated in the 1940s when some patients in the wards of Rockland State Hospital banded together to help each other get out of the hospital and to assist each other in getting jobs in the community. Once in the city, they met wherever they could—in coffee shops, at the YMCA, and on the steps of the New York Public Library. They called themselves WANA, an acronym for "We Are Not Alone." At that point, WANA had no financial backing and no professional or political sponsorship other than a few dedicated volunteers.

The members welcomed warmly into their club any patients who were discharged from mental hospitals, and they provided a support group for each other. They exchanged notes on possible jobs, helped each other find places to live, and shared problems of daily living in the community.

In mid-1948, with the help of two volunteers, the members raised enough money to buy a small four-story brownstone on West 47th Street. The volunteers and members cleaned, painted, and fixed up the house. Since there was a fountain on the patio of the old house, the club decided to call itself Fountain House.

Today 350 members use Fountain House's facilities dur-

Many homeless men and women
who roam city streets are
former mental patients.

—49—

ing the day. Members do all the clerical and housekeeping chores, prepare and serve three meals a day, run a daily newspaper, and operate a thrift shop. The emphasis is on work and on doing whatever is necessary to make the club run smoothly. Once members have mastered their jobs within the club, many of them go out into the community and are able to find work.

Fountain House's success lies in its atmosphere. The ex-patients, called members, immediately feel part of a big, extended family. They feel respected and wanted, no matter what their problems. Underlying this feeling is the expectation, "You can do it." No matter what the task, chore, or assignment, when members feel others' faith in them, they usually succeed. Consequently, their self-worth is enhanced.

Although members do not actually live at Fountain House, they can rent apartments in the area nearby so they can keep that sense of belonging. Once they are members, they belong for life. Some members keep coming back for years.

Fountain House has become the model for many other psychosocial rehabilitation programs all over the United States, such as Horizon House in Philadelphia, Thresholds in Chicago, and Fellowship House in Miami. Although each group has its own unique qualities, they all work with the chronically disabled mental patient in a community setting. Each provides a full range of services, including a rehabilitation club, a variety of living arrangements with varying degrees of supervision, and a vocational rehabilitation program. They are all transitional in nature, helping members move smoothly from institutional living to independent living in the community.

It is difficult to find anyone who would say a negative

Fountain House in New York City
is one of the most successful rehabilitation
centers for former mental patients.

word about the effectiveness of these clubs. There are now 110 clubs in operation in the United States. Many more are needed so more discharged mental patients could benefit from their services.

■ COMMUNITY
MENTAL HEALTH CENTERS
No matter where former patients live, when they move into the community, they have medical, social, and psychological needs which must be met. The community mental health centers (CMHCs), designed to replace the state hospitals, were originally planned to be the cornerstone of the deinstitutionalization movement. The centers were intended to provide the discharged patient with complete medical and psychological care near his or her home.

To receive federal funds under the law, the centers had to offer the following five services: 1) inpatient psychiatric services for full-time hospitalization at the center or at a nearby hospital, 2) emergency services twenty-four hours a day, seven days a week, 3) outpatient services, including diagnosis, evaluation, and treatment of psychiatric problems, 4) partial hospitalization services such as day, evening, or weekend treatment programs as alternatives to inpatient treatment, and 5) consultation and coordination of services with other agencies, schools, and professionals.

When the country was originally divided into catchment areas in 1963, more than 1,500 CMHCs were deemed necessary. So far, only 725 have been built. That means that in almost 800 catchment areas—over half of the country—patients are not receiving care. New York City, with some 40,000 ex-patients, has only two community mental health centers.

For many people, especially former mental patients, the centers offer a wide variety of services right in the community at a fee far lower than that of a private psychiatrist. However, if former patients live in one of the 800 catchment areas without a center, they will have to search for other community resources to meet their needs.

■ PARTIAL HOSPITALIZATION
PROGRAMS

Another resource former patients might use is a partial hospitalization program. Many patients who have left the hospital are not ready to be on their own twenty-four hours a day. Partial hospitalization programs or day treatment programs serve as a bridge between hospital living and independent living in the community. Patients who utilize these programs may have their own housing or may live with their families. They attend the programs during the day from 9 A.M. to 5 P.M. Since financial assistance will usually pay for only 120 days a year in such programs, most patients attend them three days a week.

Day treatment programs are fairly structured with an emphasis on helping former patients become more independent. Group therapy sessions try to help ex-patients understand relationships with other people and to deal with problems they encounter in daily living. There are sessions on budgeting, grooming, and auto repairs, and people may learn to cook, plan meals, enjoy arts and crafts, and play basketball or baseball. They also take field trips to different places in the community.

Many of the day treatment programs are run as democratically as possible; former patients help decide how the program runs. Staff members believe contributions from patients are crucial if the program is to reflect them and their wishes. Contributing also helps patients make decisions in their lives outside the programs. When former patients have graduated from the day treatment programs, they may go on to sheltered workshops. Here they work on projects for industries—such as stuffing boxes—within the sheltered environment of an agency rather than working directly for the company. Others go on to get jobs. In a few instances, former patients have done so well in partial hospitalization programs that they later become staff members there.

As with the other resources in the community, day treatment programs fill a real gap. Unfortunately, many more programs are needed.

■ PSYCHIATRIC UNITS IN GENERAL HOSPITALS

As we have seen, former psychiatric patients often find it necessary to return to the hospital after living for a while in the community. Today, when they have relapses, they may go to a general hospital in their own neighborhood rather than back to the mental institution. This is a relatively recent innovation. In earlier times, no one wanted "crazy" people mixing with "normal" people in a community or general hospital. They worried that the strange or wild behavior of mental patients would disturb the functioning of the hospital as a whole. Besides, mental illness was not treated medically, like a disease.

Drug therapy eliminated these reasons for keeping mental patients out of general hospitals. By the early 1970s, one general hospital in five had a separate inpatient psychiatric unit. Today more than 75 percent of hospitals with more than 500 beds have inpatient psychiatric units. Admission to these units is voluntary, and patients usually stay from two weeks to two months. If they need further treatment or turn out to be chronic cases, they may be referred to a mental hospital or institution.

For John J., a manic-depressive now working in the post office in a small midwestern town, there are many advantages to being treated in his own community hospital. When he gets depressed, about twice a year, he voluntarily admits himself to the psychiatric unit of the hospital right in his own town. There is no shame, as when he needed to go to a mental hospital. He can just tell his friends he is sick. He gets excellent medical care, since his psychiatrist collaborates with other doctors and makes referrals to medical services within the same hospital. For example, when John needed a blood test, he didn't have to get in a cab and go to another hospital, as he did when he was at the state hospital; he simply went into another part of the same hospital.

Psychiatric units in community hospitals also help reduce the stigma surrounding mental patients. When John waited for his X ray, he sat next to an orthopedic patient. As they sat and talked, the orthopedic patient learned that John was on the psychiatric ward. He was surprised to find that John was just a "regular guy," not at all "crazy" as he had imagined the mental patients to be.

Psychiatric units in general hospitals may offer the most promise of all community resources for the mentally ill because the basic facilities already exist in hospitals in cities and towns across the country. Yet almost all the resources we've examined here—particularly boarding homes, halfway houses, day treatment programs, and community health centers—suffer from a severe lack of funds for building new facilities and maintaining old ones, as well as funds for hiring enough staff members to provide the necessary services. As long as such deficiencies exist, how successful can deinstitutionalization be?

CHAPTER 5:
IS COMMUNITY
CARE WORKING?

5

From 1957 to 1977, almost 800,000 mental patients were discharged into U.S. communities that were unprepared for the onslaught. The patients, too, were unprepared for what they would find in the community. For many of them, the word "community" had no meaning at all. After spending ten or twenty years in an institution, they no longer knew anyone who lived in their old neighborhoods. They missed the security of their daily routines and the feeling of belonging they had in the hospital. Some patients, who had not been hospitalized too long, did begin to find their niche in the community, often by surrounding themselves with other former mental patients. But for hundreds of others, the question remained: would they have been better off staying in the custodial care of the state hospital?

■ A CASE STUDY
When Mary L., a 32-year-old schizophrenic, was put in a large state hospital in the south twelve years ago, she had no idea she would ever leave. Her parents were killed in a car crash two years after her admission, and she considered the hospital

her home. However, when a new law required that all patients receive the least restrictive form of treatment, Mary was designated to be discharged. She was put in an "exit group" to relearn the skills she needed to live and cope in the community.

In the hospital, Mary had become very dependent. She was given clothes and told when to put them on. She was told when to wash, where to take her bath, and when to eat her meals. She had grown fond of her daily routine; it was the one thing that never changed. Even at times when she got really angry, the other patients still accepted her.

Since everything was done for her, Mary had forgotten many skills. She didn't remember how to unlock a door, how to draw a bath, or how to open a can of soup. She had forgotten how to use a bus, how to talk to a storekeeper, and how to count money. With the help of a social worker Mary and the other patients in her exit group went on trips together into the community to practice the skills they were relearning.

After six months in the group, Mary had learned enough to leave the state hospital. Although she was proud of her progress, she told her social worker she wasn't sure if she wanted to be "here" or "there." She and six other patients were placed in a nearby boarding home where they received their room and board.

After living in the boarding home for two months, Mary started to forget to take her medication. She would forget first one day, then two days at a time. After about a week, she could not even remember where she had put the medicine bottle. Then she lost the paper on which she wrote the date of her next appointment with her social worker. At the end of three months, Mary was again hallucinating, not sleeping or eating properly, and picking fights. One day, after a fight with a friend whom she had known for three years in the hospital, she slowly walked back to the state hospital and had herself readmitted.

Like 68 percent of all discharged mental patients, Mary needed to return to the security of the hospital within a year of her discharge. Could her readmission have been prevented?

Does her readmission, and that of thousands of other patients, mean that deinstitutionalization has failed?

Opponents of deinstitutionalization point to this "revolving door syndrome" as proof that deinstitutionalization is not working. Those who favor discharging patients into the community say that repeated hospitalizations do not indicate that the system has failed. Some patients, they say, simply need to get their batteries recharged to continue living in the community.

One thing is certain: deinstitutionalization can only be as successful as the community facilities that provide care and support for former patients. How, then, are these facilities working? What problems have arisen from deinstitutionalization?

■ COMMUNITY
MENTAL HEALTH CENTERS
When President Kennedy signed the Community Mental Health Centers Act in 1963, many mental health professionals were filled with optimism that the centers would provide comprehensive outpatient services to the community at large as well as to patients discharged from mental hospitals.

Although the centers were originally built and staffed with federal money, they were expected to become self-supporting with the income received through fees that people would pay for their services. The majority of those who come to CMHCs, however, are poor people who do not have insurance and do not pay full fees. For this reason, in 1981 Congress amended the original legislation to continue federal funding for an eight year period. But this money can be cut back at any time.

Initially, physicians backed the centers, and universities supported them financially. But when they realized that the centers were not going to follow the traditional mode of therapy and were more preoccupied with public health and social and economic problems as was appropriate to their clients' needs, many physicians and universities pulled back their support.

Today the centers suffer not only from a shortage of funds but also from a shortage of personnel. Many centers are understaffed and their employees are overworked. As a result, services vary greatly from place to place. In some centers, the outpatient therapy is effective; in others, unavailable. At some centers, the emergency service is an inefficient answering service while others have a twenty-four hour hot line to handle crises. The greatest shortcoming in the centers, however, is that there simply are not enough of them to meet the demand for their services. With wide-ranging cuts in federal funding of social programs, there is likely to be little money to build additional centers. Even a number of those presently in existence may be phased out. Money has indeed become a crucial issue in community care.

■ FINANCIAL PROBLEMS

Some of the original motivation to deinstitutionalize came from the belief that care in the community would cost less than care in a mental hospital. By reducing the population in state hospitals, professionals thought funds would be freed to finance less restrictive outpatient services in the community. Although the actual cost of an individual's care has in some cases been reduced, the savings have not been passed on to community services.

Money remains one of the most important factors in care for the chronic mental patient, and one professional after another repeats the same problem: "The states have not found a way for money to follow the mental patient from the psychiatric hospital to the community." This has not been done either

In a therapeutic workshop at a
Community Mental Health Center,
discharged mental patients
learn woodworking skills.

on a patient-by-patient basis or on a larger scale. With high rates of inflation and reductions in government spending, many mental health professionals are concerned that there is not enough money to finance the services that would help former mental patients survive in the community. The lack of funds raises a fundamental question. Whose responsibility is it to finance the halfway house, the job training program, or the sheltered workshop?

Legislation must be passed in order to make public funds available. Yet leadership has not materialized at the federal, state, or local levels. Legislators are often guided more by political considerations than by clinical needs. They will give money to a vocal visible group rather than to a quiet, needy one, like the mentally ill. Since they are often overburdened with their own individual problems, these people do not have the confidence to stand up for their needs as a group. As a result, their political influence is miniscule, and funds for programs are slow in coming.

■ COMMUNITY RESISTANCE
Another obstacle to successful deinstitutionalization lies in the community's attitude toward individuals who have been hospitalized in mental institutions. At a general level, the public's attitude is reflected in its reluctance to make mental health a priority concern, so that money might be available for improving community care.

On a more personal level, the community's prejudices and misconceptions about former patients are shown in the results of a survey done by the National Association of Private Psychiatric Hospitals: "One-quarter of a population recently surveyed would not want people who have had mental health problems as neighbors, while 60 percent would not want them as tenants. Former psychiatric patients have trouble getting housing, credit, insurance, and licenses."

If a community has rigid standards of dress, someone who dresses sloppily, does not smell clean, or wears old, outdated clothes will stand out as different. People are afraid of those who look different. If they look different, they wonder, will they also act differently?

When people notice that the man who recently took a one-room apartment in the neighborhood is also muttering to himself and picking through the neighbors' garbage on trash collection day, they become afraid. Perhaps one day he may become agitated if he doesn't find what he wants in the trash and strike out and hurt someone.

The major problem for most mental patients is their inability to face the world, not their desire to attack it. Yet the public continues to see former mental patients as dangerous. Part of the reason for this impression goes back to the days when mental hospitals were seen as prisons for the mentally ill. Today this impression may be reinforced by an increasing number of violent crimes—mass murders, assassination attempts, senseless shootings and assaults—committed by people who are severely disturbed. Research, however, has proven that less than 2 percent of all patients discharged from mental hospitals get in trouble with the law.

Unfortunately, mental health professionals are unable to predict which patients will, in fact, turn out to be dangerous. For this reason, the public's uncertainty and fear about how ex-patients will act cannot entirely be put to rest.

■ THE PROFESSIONAL'S ROLE

Even professionals who work in the field of mental health are not completely free of negative attitudes toward people who are severely disturbed. Social workers, psychiatrists, and psychologists often consider the mentally ill difficult to treat, uninteresting, and even frightening. Since many former patients have poor records for keeping appointments and following up on their medication, work with them can be frustrating and difficult.

In addition, many ex-patients are involved with three or four social agencies at once. Each agency has its own social workers with their own functions. For example, when Sara K. was discharged from the state hospital, she moved into a halfway house. There she joined a group, run by a social worker, to help her learn how to get along with other young people. Twice a month she checked in with another social worker who saw that she got her welfare check. Sara also stopped periodically at the community mental health center to have her medication monitored and to talk with the social worker there about how things were going. Each agency had its own records and procedures as well as its own funding. Consequently, coordinating the services of the three agencies involved in Sara's case was almost impossible.

■ DRUG ABUSE
In addition to keeping track of all her appointments with social workers, living in the community presented another problem for Sara. After about a month in the halfway house, Sara had made a couple of friends with whom she ate her meals. Since she was taking her medication regularly by herself, she didn't see any need to go back to the CMHC to have her medication checked. One day, after a fight with one of her new friends, Sara started to feel confused; she couldn't think straight. When she went to take her medicine, she couldn't remember how much to take. Since there were only a few tablets left in the bottle, she decided to finish it off. The next thing Sara remembered was finding herself in the emergency room of the local hospital with a drug overdose.

According to a study done at Massachusetts General Hospital between 1962 and 1975, 7 percent of all overdose cases result from antipsychotic drugs. While this is not a high percentage, it still represents a problem. When ex-mental patients take drugs outside of the hospital, they must be closely monitored. Taking too much medication is just as serious and dangerous as not taking medication at all, a situation that can also land former patients back in the hospital.

■ ARE THERE ANY
SUCCESS STORIES?
Many patients who have been discharged into the community live there for the rest of their lives. For example, four women

patients left an eastern state hospital at the same time and set up an apartment together. None of them have been able to give up their hallucinations or delusions, yet they cook, shop, and clean their apartment. They help each other stay on their medication; they go together to the CMHC to see their social workers. Three have stayed on welfare, but one was able to get a job as a clerk in a local store. Together, they form a family unit.

Sam left a state hospital in the West at age 32. Although he had spent fifteen years there, he never picked up the institutionalized trappings, such as shuffling feet and nervous tics. He has now been out of the hospital for ten years without a readmission. He made it because he had a family to go home to, attended a clinic regularly, and stayed on his medication. Sam also had a "teddy bear" quality about him that made people like him even though at times the neighbors thought he acted a little strange.

There are many more examples of former patients who have made it in communities all over the country, but a common thread runs through all of these successful cases. They each stayed on their medication and used it as directed, even when they may have felt it wasn't helping or they didn't really need it. They also had good support systems: people around them who cared about them and who helped them when they needed it. Research has also shown that generally patients who have spent less time in institutions adjust more easily to life in the community.

■ MUST IT BE EITHER/OR?
The tendency in the past was to look at care for the mentally ill in an either/or fashion. Either all the mentally ill are cared for in mental hospitals, as was the case for hundreds of years, or they are all discharged into the community, as happened in the early 1960s. The mentally ill, however, cannot be lumped together as one uniform group. What is good for one patient may not be right for another. Each patient is an individual with his or her own problems and strengths, reactions and emotions.

For some patients, deinstitutionalization can and does work. But for others who have lived more years in the hospital than in the community, deinstitutionalization will never be a reality. Professionals are now beginning to realize that they would be doing patients a disservice by moving them into the community after they have been hospitalized for twenty to forty years.

Many chronic patients will never learn to count money to buy a bottle of milk at the corner store. They cannot understand how to use a laundromat to wash their clothes. They do not know how to dial a phone. After years in the state hospital, these patients, who have long had an "institutional look," will always need care in a secure and protected environment. The state hospital, like the custodial care institution of the past, must again be considered an option to provide permanent care for these homeless people.

CHAPTER 6:
LEGAL RIGHTS

6

Kenneth Donaldson, a 48-year-old carpenter and the divorced father of three children, paid his parents a visit in 1957. While he was there, he complained of harrassment by unknown people. Since he had had a previous nervous breakdown, his father became worried about him and had him committed to Florida State Hospital at Chattahoochee, where there were 500 patients to one doctor. He was forced to live for fourteen years with seriously disturbed patients, including criminals, in a locked sixty-bed ward and was given no psychiatric treatment.

During his hospitalization, Donaldson repeatedly made petitions for his freedom, which were ignored. Finally, in 1970, he filed a suit on behalf of himself and other patients demanding to be treated or released and awarded damages. He was discharged the following year, but the damage claim kept the case alive longer. He later received $38,000 in personal damages from two psychiatrists, one of whom was Dr. O'Connor, clinical director and later superintendent of the state hospital. In 1975, the Supreme Court heard the now famous *O'Connor v. Donaldson* case and ruled that every nondangerous mental patient who is institutionalized against his will has the right to be treated or discharged.

This case does not represent an isolated incident of a patient standing up for his legal rights, but prior to the 1970s, very few patients or concerned individuals were willing to speak out for the injustices done to people who are mentally disturbed. Louis Kopolow, M.D., Chief of Patients' Rights and Advocacy in the Mental Health Services division of the National Institute of Mental Health, points out this shift. "There is a change in pattern: we always had some exposé occur, but now the mental health system is continuing under the spotlight for at least ten years."

■ PATIENTS' RIGHTS MOVEMENT

The thrust for patients' rights in the field of mental health began in the 1960s under President Kennedy with the general concern for social causes. The civil rights movement led lawyers to look into prison conditions, since most of the inmates were black. From the prisons, the next logical target for young, socially conscious lawyers was the mental institution. There they found a population that was both passive and easy to champion. Unlike criminals, the mentally ill had done nothing wrong. Yet they were warehoused in custodial, prison-like facilities and treated like criminals.

These lawyers were supported by ex-patient groups, some of which have helped clarify some of the issues involved. They are particularly concerned with the civil rights of people society sees as mentally ill. These groups seek freedom for the mentally ill to exercise their full human rights, not only their right to be patients. Their cause often conflicts with opinions held by many mental health professionals. In his article, "Consumer Demands in Mental Health Care" in the *International Journal of Law and Psychiatry*, Dr. Kopolow explains, "Ex-patient groups strongly disagree with the two principal arguments usually raised by mental health professionals in defense of involuntary treatment—the issue of dangerousness, and the assumption that most patients with emotional problems are incompetent to know what they need and thus, cannot be permitted to make their own decisions."

A great deal has been written about whether mental health professionals are able to predict the dangerousness of mental patients. In *An ACLU Handbook: The Rights of Mental Patients*, Bruce J. Ennis and Richard D. Emery write, "Despite the popular belief to the contrary, it now seems beyond dispute that mental health professionals have *no* expertise in predicting future dangerous behavior, either to self or to others. In fact, predictions of dangerous behavior are wrong about 95 percent of the time." Even with those mental patients who have a history of dangerous behavior in the recent past, predictions are wrong two-thirds of the time. Thus, if people are committed on the basis of wrong predictions, many harmless individuals will be put in institutions.

■ A VULNERABLE MINORITY
The mentally ill are a unique minority, and according to Dr. Kopolow, they are unusually vulnerable. They have problems thinking clearly, articulating what they want and, especially, being heard as individuals with something to say. Therefore, they need an advocate, someone to help protect their rights.

Everyone has been in a similar position of vulnerability. For example, when Marcia M.'s car breaks down, she is at the mercy of the car mechanic. He probably knows more about cars than she does and is in a position to take advantage of her lack of knowledge. Yet, vulnerability in this one area does not mean that Marcia is totally incompetent.

Likewise, mental illness does not cover all areas of functioning. It is not the same as incompetence. People who are mentally ill can still tell you that they do not like to sleep with the lights on all night or that they feel better using some medications than others.

In the past, psychiatrists believed that patients, because they were mentally ill, did not know what was best for them and that the psychiatrists must act for the patients, in their behalf. This was not an advocate role, but more the role of a protective parent acting for an incapable child. Some mental illnesses, because of their nature, *do* prevent the patient from knowing whether he or she needs help. But in many other cases, patients have the right, as human beings, to say whether they prefer their freedom to being in an institution.

■ OBJECTIONS TO INVOLUNTARY COMMITMENT

In the past, it was considered necessary to commit patients to mental hospitals to protect the patients from themselves as well as to protect the community from them. Now this is being questioned. Ex-patient groups oppose involuntary commitment or forced hospitalization for any reason. Others, especially some psychiatrists, believe that at certain points, when patients are no longer rational, they have the right to expect someone to recognize their need, to protect them from their own lack of reason, and to take care of them.

If a man claims that his room is filled with man-eating snakes and that he must jump out of the twelfth-story window to avoid them, should he be protected? Or if a woman is convinced, because of the irrational aspect of her illness, that she is a divine bird and is ready to fly off the roof of her house, should she be cared for? Our commitment laws try to compromise these two conflicting principles: protection of individual freedom and caring for those who are sick.

It is difficult to generalize about how people are committed to mental institutions because there are wide differences among the states' laws. In addition, laws are changing very rapidly. According to *An ACLU Handbook: The Rights of Mental Patients,* "The clear trend is to require proof of overt acts, threats, or attempts of a dangerous nature in the recent past, and to prohibit involuntary hospitalization if 'need for treatment' is the only reason for hospitalization."

In the past, patients had no way of objecting to being involuntarily hospitalized. But after the recent flurry of court decisions with the emphasis on patients' rights, the situation changed. It is now recognized that the constitutional doctrine of "least restrictive alternative" applies to the mental health field. This means that no one can be committed to a state or private mental hospital if there are other methods of treat-

A patient in a mental hospital discusses his problems with the resident psychologist as part of his treatment plan.

ment that restrain his or her personal freedom less. Within the mental hospital, patients can be transferred from a locked unit to an open one, and their rights can be constitutionally upheld. In short, forced treatment in a mental hospital is unconstitutional if the same purpose can be achieved by treating the patient in an outpatient facility or in a halfway house in the community.

■ RIGHT TO TREATMENT

If it is decided that hospitalization *is* the least restrictive alternative, then those patients who are hospitalized deserve to be treated. This sounds obvious to us today, but for decades, mental patients were housed in large hospitals with only custodial care. That is, they received shelter and protection, but no psychiatric treatment as we know it today.

The first person to recognize this discrepancy was Dr. Morton Birnbaum, an attorney and physician who suggested in 1960 in the *American Bar Association Journal* that people who were involuntarily committed to mental institutions have a "right to treatment." At that time, his idea was received with interest but no action was taken.

Ten years later, in 1970, the Supreme Court ruled in the *O'Connor v. Donaldson* case that a finding of "mental illness" alone cannot justify a state's indefinitely locking up people against their wills and giving them only custodial care. They found no constitutional basis for confining individuals involuntarily if they are dangerous to no one and can live safely in freedom.

■ RIGHT TO REFUSE TREATMENT

Diabetics can refuse to take insulin, heart patients can refuse digitalis, and certain religious groups can refuse to receive blood transfusions. Their right to refuse these treatments is protected by both criminal and civil law. Then why can't a mental patient refuse ECT or an antipsychotic drug?

John Rennie, an airplane pilot and flight instructor in New Jersey, developed severe psychotic symptoms after the death of his twin brother in an airplane accident. Diagnosed as a paranoid schizophrenic, he was admitted and discharged from a mental institution twelve times over a three-year period. After threatening to assassinate President Ford, he was again taken into custody by the Secret Service and admitted to a mental hospital.

While hospitalized, he was forced to take antipsychotic medication, Prolixin Hydrochloride. His condition improved dramatically, but he began to suffer some of the drug's side effects, including early signs of tardive dyskinesia.

In December 1977, Mr. Rennie obtained a temporary restraining order from Federal District Judge Stanley Brotman to discontinue his medication. Brotman ruled that "forced antipsychotic medication in nonemergency situations violates the constitutional right to privacy," according to the January 26, 1981 issue of the *National Law Journal*. Several days after the decision, however, Mr. Rennie's condition deteriorated, and he needed Thorazine on an emergency basis. Judge Brotman modified his restraining order to allow certain medication to be given. He felt that Rennie was not able at that time to participate meaningfully in his treatment decision.

Although Rennie lost his original case, he did help other New Jersey mental patients in 1979 when he brought a class action suit against the hospital administrators. In this second case, *Rennie* v. *Klein*, Judge Brotman reaffirmed his earlier decision. He ruled that in any nonemergency situation, a hearing was necessary before a patient could be given drugs against his or her will. In 1981, however, this case was still being appealed.

Other judges in Massachusetts and Ohio have made similar rulings. These decisions do not sit well with some members of the psychiatric profession. When Boston's Judge Joseph L. Tauro made a similar ruling in 1979, American Psychiatric Association President Alan Stone called it "the most impossible, inappropriate, ill-considered judicial decision in the field of mental health law." Like Dr. Stone, some psychiatrists have a different view of what is good for the patient. This type of decision, they believe, reduces their authority to decide whether patients should be medicated, even against their will.

At issue are the patient's rights to privacy and independence versus the hospital's obligations to provide treatment and to protect the patients from themselves and from each other.

If a patient knows that a particular treatment method is only 60 percent effective and has a long list of side effects, is he irrational to refuse to take it? Do patients, regardless of how sick they are, have a right to know what they're getting? While physicians generally uphold their belief in informed consent, some argue that if they disclosed all the side effects of every medication, no one would ever take any medicine.

■ EX-PATIENT GROUPS

Some of the most vocal advocates of the patient's right to refuse treatment are former patients themselves. Motivated by their negative experiences with psychiatrists, drugs, and mental hospitals, they started banding together in the early 1970s to fight for their rights. In Cambridge, Massachusetts, they are called Mental Patients' Liberation Front; in Santa Monica, California, they are Network Against Psychiatric Assault; in Philadelphia, Pennsylvania, the Alliance for the Liberation of Mental Patients. More than twenty-five of these groups form a national network, but they are in no way unified in what they believe or in how they act.

Some groups that follow the footsteps of Dr. Thomas Szasz are opposed to the concept of mental illness and favor nonprofessional, nonmedical alternatives to mental health care. Others are self-help groups that meet quietly every week to support members who are former psychiatric patients. Still others, such as Project Overcome in Minneapolis, Minnesota, are working to minimize the stigma surrounding mental illness.

At the far end of the spectrum are the radical political advocacy groups of ex-patients, whose activities sometimes speak more clearly than their words. At one point, The Alliance for Liberation of Mental Patients boycotted SmithKline Corporation, the developer of the antipsychotic drug Thorazine, by urging people to stop buying their over-the-counter drugs. In its quarterly journal, *Madness Network News, Inc.*,

Network Against Psychiatric Assault published a "Shock Doctor Roster," a list of all the physicians in the country who administer ECT. This was in response to some psychiatric facilities that post "Shock Rosters," naming patients who are to receive ECT at a certain time.

Many psychiatrists ignore these groups or dismiss them as insignificant. Some of the more radical groups are accused of hurting the entire cause by being too noisy and too inflexible about what they are against, rather than standing up for what they believe in. Although ex-patient groups may not play a significant part in changing the laws, they are an important force in trying to make the mental health system more responsive to patients' needs. They also serve to raise the public consciousness to a greater awareness of mental patients as people with feelings and rights.

■ ADVOCACY WITHIN
THE HOSPITAL
Within the mental hospital, too, patients are standing up for their rights as human beings to be treated humanely. More and more state and private hospitals have patient advocacy groups that help patients ask for basic things, such as flexible bedtimes and air conditioning for their rooms. In addition, human rights committees—comprised of patients, staff members, and community people—investigate patients' complaints of mistreatment, cruelty, or harrassment within the hospital.

■ FAMILIES UNITE
As hard as patients and ex-patients are fighting for their rights, especially their right to refuse treatment, another group is battling just as hard for the patient's right to receive treatment. The mothers, fathers, and spouses of people who are mentally ill have seen what happens when their children or husbands or wives do not receive the medication they need. As we have seen, some patients who are mentally ill will deny being sick and refuse medication. Often it is their families who bear the brunt of their abuse, taunts, and threats when they refuse to seek help.

Because of their personal nightmares, family members of the mentally ill have formed groups to support each other. Beginning in the late 1970s, families of the mentally ill started to shed some of their anger that this could happen to them and their guilt over responsibility for the illness. Once they did this, they could talk openly about personal traumas, and about their disturbed children's and spouses' need for treatment. They found that they were not alone. As families talked more publicly, others joined and shared their personal experiences.

Besides giving each other emotional support, family groups also advocate stricter commitment laws, better after-care facilities, and more liberal insurance coverage for the mentally ill. Grass-roots groups of this nature formed simultaneously all over the country. In the fall of 1979, groups from more than twenty-eight states joined forces and formed the National Alliance for the Mentally Ill, Inc. This national organization helps new groups get started, lobbies in Congress for mental health legislation that supports their goals, and sponsors a national conference annually.

As with most questions that involve a number of points of view, the issue of legal rights is very complex. Psychiatrists and lawyers, as well as patients and their families, often set the issues from different perspectives. And there are no easy answers, no single right and wrong approach, because individual cases vary so widely. In the end, protecting the rights of the patient is a kind of balancing act in which the patient's civil rights must be weighed against the responsibility of medical professionals to care for the ill.

CHAPTER 7:
CONCLUSION

7

People who are mentally ill have long been a forgotten minority. For decades they have been forgotten inside custodial care institutions. They have been pushed into communities before they were ready and shunted into single rooms in dilapidated neighborhoods. Many times, it is we, the people of the community, who wish to forget the mentally ill because they may appear different from us.

The reaction of people in the community to seriously disturbed individuals has influenced the kind of care they have received for hundreds of years. We have looked at different methods of care and treatment in state and private hospitals, in boarding homes and halfway houses. We have seen the delicate balance between the patient's right to independence and autonomy and society's desire to care for those who are sick. We have sensed, too, the patient's ambivalence and anguish about whether he or she belongs in a hospital or in the community.

The questions of how to care for the mentally ill remain complex. Will deinstitutionalization prove to be the best solution to the problem, in spite of its shortcomings? Or is this concept too idealistic to survive in a society where money to support social services is in short supply and great demand? Do our attitudes toward the mentally ill prevent our offering them the help they need to live in the community? To what extent can mental patients be consulted about where they want to live? And what about the treatment of the illness itself? Does society have a responsibility to provide medical treatment for the mentally ill? Does a patient have a right to refuse that treatment? And what is a doctor's responsibility to a patient who cannot make decisions about his or her treatment?

From this book, it is hoped that the reader has gained compassion for those individuals who are severely disturbed, as well as an understanding of the complexity of issues and options involved in caring for the mentally ill.

GLOSSARY

anxiety—a state of uneasiness, apprehension, or worry.

asylum—a mental institution.

behavior modification—a method of changing behavior by rewarding or reinforcing certain habits.

boarding home—any type of residential living facility which provides food and shelter for a fee to unrelated adults.

catchment area—a defined geographic area.

cathartic method—a technique in which emotional tension is released by talking about material that had formerly been unconscious.

community mental health center (CMHC)—a public or private nonprofit entity through which comprehensive mental health services are provided to people living within a catchment area.

custodial care—shelter and protection within a mental hospital.

deinstitutionalization—discharging patients from state and county mental institutions into the community.

delusion—a persistent false belief.

depression—extreme sadness, dejection, and a feeling of worthlessness.

free association—a technique in psychotherapy in which patients talk freely about whatever comes into their conscious minds.

hallucination—perceiving something that does not exist in reality.

manic-depression—a mental disorder characterized by severe mood swings between elation and depression.

outpatient—a person who is receiving services or treatment in a clinic or hospital, but is not hospitalized.

psychoanalysis—a theory of personality development and a method of psychotherapy, based on the work of Sigmund Freud.

psychosis—a severe mental disturbance in which the person is grossly out of touch with reality.

psychotherapy—a method of treatment for people with emotional problems.

schizophrenia—a group of psychoses marked by bizarre behavior, hallucinations, and delusions.

tardive dyskinesia—a side effect from antipsychotic medication which causes permanent damage to the part of the brain that is used to control and coordinate muscle movement.

FOR FURTHER READING

Ennis, Bruce J., and Emery, Richard D. *An American Civil Liberties Union Handbook: The Rights of Mental Patients.* New York: Avon Books, 1978.

Friedburg, John. M.D. *Shock Treatment is Not Good for Your Brain.* San Francisco: Glide Publications, 1976.

Langone, John. *Goodbye to Bedlam: Understanding Mental Illness and Retardation.* Boston/Toronto: Little Brown and Co., 1974.

Milt, Harry. *Basic Handbook of Mental Illness.* New York: Charles Scribner's Sons, 1974.

Park, Clara Claiborne, and Shapiro, Leon N., M.D. *You Are Not Alone: Understanding and Dealing with Mental Illness.* Boston/Toronto: Little Brown and Co., 1976.

Steir, Charles. *Blue Jolts: True Stories from the Cuckoo's Nest.* Washington, D.C.: New Republic Books, 1978.

Viscott, David S., M.D. *The Making of a Psychiatrist.* Greenwich, Conn.: Fawcett Publications, 1972.

INDEX